THE MUSLIM
PARENT'S GUIDE
TO THE EARLY YEARS
(0-5 YEARS)

Umm Safiyyah bint Najmaddin

Ta-Ha Publishers Ltd.

© 1431 AH/2010 CE Ta-Ha Publishers Ltd.
First Published in February 2011
Reprinted: 2012 and 2013

Ta-Ha Publishers Ltd.
Unit 4, The Windsor Centre
Windsor Grove, West Norwood
London, SE27 9NT, UK
www.tahapublishers.com

Written by: Umm Safiyyah bint Najmaddin
Edited by: Dr. Abia Afsar-Siddiqui
Cover/Book Design by: Shakir Abdulcadir » opensquares.co.uk

A catalogue record of this book is available from the British Library
ISBN 978 1 84200 122 6

Printed and bound by: IMAK Ofset, TURKEY

CONTENTS

In the Name of Allah,
the Most Gracious, the Most Merciful

INTRODUCTION

All praises are due to Allah 🕮, Lord of the *'Alameen* (all that exists), may the peace and blessings of Allah 🕮 be upon His Prophet Muhammad 🕮, his family, his Companions and those that follow righteous guidance, ameen.

How can I keep my pre-school age child stimulated at home? What activities can I do with them? What is the best way of teaching them? How do I handle a disruptive child? These are just a few of the questions parents have asked me during my years of working with young children.

A contented, confident and well-adjusted child does not come about by accident but is the result of hard work mainly on the part of the parents. It is not enough to send our children to nursery and expect teachers to do our job for us. Primary education comes from the home environment and the first and best teachers are parents themselves. As Muslim parents in a non-Muslim society, we have to work hard to ensure that Islam is the focus of our parenting efforts.

The pre-school years are the most important and rapid stage of development, so this is a golden opportunity for us to nurture our children and help them on the path to becoming good Muslims of the future. It is a grave mistake to think that children are too young to learn or understand their surroundings. In fact the opposite is true; the younger the child, the faster they can absorb information. A lack of varied stimuli and unsettled emotional surroundings are major factors in disruptive behaviour.

There is a wealth of literature about bringing up children, all of which have their merits and wisdoms. When reading these books, it is important to ensure that we take only that which is within the bounds of the teachings of Allah and His Messenger ﷺ. There are, however, few books written specifically for parents from the Islamic perspective.

This book is aimed at both mothers and fathers and is a guide to help bring up pre-school age children in an Islamic setting. I draw upon my experience as a mother and techniques learnt from my time as a nursery nurse to explain how to handle everyday situations, how to engage with our children and how to help them to achieve their potential.

We all want the best for our children but often either do not know where to start or cannot find the time to implement our intentions. I hope this book will be helpful in providing suggestions about how to get started as well as highlighting that the simplest and easiest changes can have a great impact on the lives of our children. I have tried to base as much as possible on the Qur'an and *Sunnah*, and any mistakes are my own. I do not deal with the period after birth or the *fiqh* relating to children, but rather offer practical suggestions that can be implemented into our daily lives.

> *Each of you is a shepherd and each of you is responsible for his flock. The leader is a shepherd and is responsible for his flock; a man is the shepherd of his family and is responsible for his flock; a women is the shepherd in the house of her husband and is responsible for it. Each of you is a shepherd and is responsible for his flock.* (Bukhari and Muslim)

umm safiyyah
April 2010

CHAPTER ONE

THE ROLE OF PARENTS

As parents you will play a central role throughout your child's life, but more especially during the formative years when there are fewer external influences. It is important, therefore, that you try to develop good habits and positive behaviours as early as possible, so as to be able to impart these to your child and help create an environment in which they can flourish. This chapter highlights the main issues to consider and subsequent chapters will develop and expand on these themes.

✏ UNDERSTAND YOUR CHILD

Allah has created every individual with a unique personality and character traits. Each child has different strengths and develops at a different pace, with some benefitting from a certain teaching style more than another. Even siblings are different from each other. In order for you as parents, and especially mothers, to be effective in your role as primary carers and educators, it is important that you recognise this and work to develop a deep understanding of the nature of your own child. This requires spending time with them and paying attention to their abilities, likes and dislikes. By investing your time and attention in your child in this way, you will be rewarded with a fulfilling parent-child relationship that helps to bring out the best in them, now and in the future.

✏ DON'T LET YOUR CHILD RULE YOU!

It is essential to create clear boundaries and rules about what is acceptable behaviour and what is not. The principles of Islam will provide the basic framework for these rules, and it is your responsibility to make your child aware of the commands of Allah and to enjoin what is good and forbid what is evil.

> **O ye who believe! Save yourselves and your families from a fire whose fuel is man and stones...**
> (Surah at-Tahrim 66:6)

Ensure that you strike a balance. If you are over-demanding and expect too much from your child, then they will not have confidence in their abilities. However, if you don't have a rule structure for your child then they can end up being disruptive. If your child does overstep the boundaries, maintain your calm, be reasonable, tell them that their behaviour is not acceptable and explain why. This helps them to learn and insha'Allah not repeat it. The key is to be consistent with the boundaries that you have set and in your explanations to your child.

✏ BE A GOOD ROLE MODEL

From a young age, babies and children imitate their parents, therefore you will need to be aware of your behaviour and moral conduct and constantly make the effort to improve your character. You may think your child does not understand or is even aware of your behaviour, when in fact they are already learning instinctively from the moment they are born. The simplest way to ensure that your child behaves as you would like them to is by leading with your own example. And by far the best example to follow is that of the Prophet Muhammad ﷺ. It is reported that A'ishah ﷞ said:

> "Whenever Fatimah came into the room, the Prophet would stand up, welcome her, kiss her and offer her his seat, and whenever he came into the room, she would stand up, take his hand, welcome him, kiss him and offer him her seat. When she came to see him during the final illness, he welcomed her and kissed her."
> (Bukhari and Muslim)

SubhanAllah, this *hadith* demonstrates how the Prophet ﷺ was a real parent and a real role model. How often do we see this level of etiquette directed towards our children today?

➥ JOIN IN

Children love to play and they will appreciate you joining in and playing with them whatever their age rather than leaving them on their own or in front of the TV for any length of time. If you have more than one child, of course they will benefit from playing with each other, but it is important to allow each child time alone with you as well. It is easy to neglect this aspect of parenting when you have a huge number of day-to-day responsibilities and playing with children can sometimes be low down on the list of priorities. However, it is essential that you manage your duties in such a way as to devote quality time to your child. The Prophet ﷺ used to line up 'Abdullah, 'Ubaydullah and Kuthayyir, the sons of Al-Abbas, and say:

> "Whoever reaches me first, I will give him such-and-such." So they would race towards him and jump on his back and chest, kissing him. (Ahmad)

There are several benefits of playing with your child. Not only are there many lessons that you can teach them through play, you can also develop an understanding of your child through the way they react. Over time, you can gauge what their skills, abilities and preferences are and how these develop. You can build on their strengths and help develop their weaknesses, thus insha'Allah creating well-rounded individuals. In short, learn how your child learns.

✏ PRAISE AND VALUE YOUR CHILD

It is all too easy in the rush of life to notice only your child's negative behaviour, pick up on it and tell them off. However, done constantly, this can be damaging to their self-esteem both as a child and as an adult. Instead, make a point of noticing the positive things that your child does, however simple, such as painting you a picture, picking up their clothes or putting their plate in the sink. Make sure they know you appreciate it by using words such as *masha'Allah* and *jazakAllah*.

Make *du'a* for them to remain amongst the righteous ones and ask Allah for His mercy upon them. Narrated Usama bin Zaid ؓ:

> "Allah's Messenger used to put me on (one of) his thighs and put Al-Hasan bin 'Ali on his other thigh, and then embrace us and say, 'O Allah! Please be Merciful to them, as I am merciful to them.'" (Bukhari)

By praising a child, it not only boosts their self-esteem but also strongly affects their behaviour throughout their adolescence and adulthood. They are far more able to achieve to the best of their ability if they have the confidence in themselves to be able to do so.

✏ SHOW AFFECTION

Of course you know that you love your child but it is not enough to just work hard and make sacrifices for them. You must be demonstrative with your affections. In other words, kiss, hug and hold your child. It is the best and easiest way of making them feel loved and secure. A child who is shown affection will respond by being respectful and affectionate towards you as well. No matter how busy you may be, always receive your child's hugs and kisses with a show of pleasure and encouragement because there are few things as pure and beautiful as the love of an innocent child. Over indulging your child with gifts is not a substitute for a real show of affection and will only lead to making your child materialistic at a later age. A simple smile, hug or 'I love you' is far more precious. Abu Hurayrah ﷺ said:

> *"The Prophet kissed Al-Hasan ibn 'Ali, and Al-Aqra' ibn Habis said: 'I have ten children, and I have never kissed any of them.' The Prophet said, 'He who does not show mercy will not be shown mercy.'"*
> (Bukhari and Muslim)

✏ COMMUNICATE WITH YOUR CHILD

One of the most successful ways of achieving a good relationship with your child is effective communication. Ensure that you speak to them with love and kindness rather than talking down to them. Be calm in your manner and exercise patience. They, too, will be calm and patient, insha'Allah. It is important not to be quick to lose your temper or take out your own frustrations on your child. After all, they are still learning so it is better to forgive their little misdemeanours. Instead, play with them, tell them you love them, hug them and smile with them. Show an interest in what they are interested in and share with them what you are interested in.

Remember that the Prophet ﷺ always smiled. Try smiling instead of frowning and you will see the difference on your child's face and the effect on their heart. In fact, try it with other children and adults as well. You will feel better for it! Anas ﷺ reported:

"Whenever the Prophet passed by a group of boys he would smile fondly and greet them."
(Bukhari and Muslim)

IN SHORT:

- Take time to interact with your child and get to know them.

- Ensure that there are rules and boundaries in place.

- Be aware of your own behaviour and actions.

- Use positive and respectful language when speaking to your child.

- Praise your child's achievements.

- Show affection to your child and receive their affection with pleasure.

- When your child talks to you, take the time to listen with interest.

CHAPTER TWO

CREATING AN ISLAMIC HOME

The home is the child's first school, so it is important to create an environment that will support their physical, mental, emotional and spiritual development and allow them to be confident and contented young people. The home environment is not just about the physical way that the home is set up but also the general atmosphere that exists between the members of the household. By ensuring that your home is a happy place, where goodness and positive actions are encouraged, it will be a place where you all enjoy spending time together as a family, insha'Allah.

✏ SALAH

Allah created us to worship Him alone; it is the purpose of our lives. So, we should fill our homes with worship. Children will naturally imitate the actions and words that they see and hear, and older children may ask what you are doing. In response, you can explain that Allah has given us so many wonderful blessings that we worship Him as a way of saying thank you. Even for babies, it is worth repeating simple words such as *Allahu Akbar* out loud to them. Allow older children to join in with you if they wish to but do not tell them off if they would rather play. Remember that *salah* is only obligatory from the age of seven, but it is not a bad idea to set a strong foundation earlier than this.

You can encourage your child to perform *salah* by:
» Praying in the presence of your children;
» Explaining to them why we pray;
» Letting them pick out their "special" prayer mat;
» Showing them the direction to pray and explaining this with pictures of the *Ka'bah*;
» Giving them a compass to find the *Qiblah*;
» Praying in a group, as a family or with other children;
» Encouraging and praising them when they do pray, even if it is not perfect.

It is also important not to make *salah* feel like a chore that takes the child away from their fun activities. If you view *salah* positively and look forward to it as a means of spiritual refreshment, then your child will pick up on this attitude as well. These are just two of the many quotes about the benefits of *salah* from the Qur'an and *hadith*:

And establish regular prayers at the two ends of the day and at the approaches of the night: for those things that are good remove those that are evil...
(Surah Hud 11:114)

Jabir ﷺ said, "The Messenger of Allah ﷺ said:
'The five daily prayers are like a deep river flowing by the door of any of you, in which he bathes five times each day.'" (Muslim)

➾ QUR'AN

The importance of reading, reciting and/or listening to the Qur'an every day cannot be over-emphasised. This will bring peace and tranquillity to your heart and your home as well as warding off evil. The Messenger of Allah ﷺ said:
"Do not make your houses into graves. The Shaytan flees from a house in which Surah al-Baqarah is recited." (Muslim)

"Verily he who has nothing of the Qur'an in his heart, is like a house (which has been) destroyed." (At-Tirmidhi)

It is never too early to introduce your child to the Qur'an so that it becomes part of their nature and they feel incomplete without it. Alhamdulillah, there are many ways to easily incorporate the Qur'an in our lives from a variety of beautiful Qur'ans for all ages, CDs and internet downloads. The following suggestions will help to you to encourage your child to adopt the Qur'an as a part of their daily life:

» Recite or put on an audio of the Qur'an in the presence of your child, in the home as well as the car. Insha'Allah, they will slowly memorise it without even realising.

» Instead of singing nursery rhymes before bedtime, recite from the Qur'an. There are several *ahadith* about what is recommended to be read at bedtime including the last three *quls*, *Ayat al-Kursi*, the last two verses of *Surah al-Baqarah*, *Surah as-Sajdah* and *Surah al-Mulk*.

» Always keep a Qur'an to hand with you. Read from it, refer to it when you are searching for the answer to a question or just when you need to seek solace. Your child will start to imitate you.

» Take your older child with you to the Islamic bookshop and allow them to choose an easy-to-read Qur'an for themselves. Teach them how to respect it and look after it.

» Make time at least once every day to sit together and read, even if it is just one *ayah*. The best time is when your child is mentally fresh and eager to learn, for example, early in the morning.

» Take the time to explain more about the Qur'an to your child. For example, tell them what an *ayah* is or what a *surah* is; how the Qur'an was revealed; how it was compiled etc. This will keep them interested and motivated.

➪ SADAQAH

Sadaqah increases the *iman* and erases sins and can be done easily by anyone, young or old, rich or poor. As the Prophet Muhammad ﷺ explained, it is not just about giving money, it is any good deed:

> *"To smile in the company of your brother is charity. To command to do good deeds and to prevent others from doing evil is charity. To guide a person in a place where he cannot get astray is charity. To remove troublesome things like thorns and bones from the road is charity. To pour water from your jug into the jug of your brother is charity. To guide a person with defective vision is charity for you."* (Bukhari)

Impress upon your child the importance of *sadaqah*. Point out to them opportunities to gain the rewards of Allah and they will soon, insha'Allah, grow to be kind, unselfish, caring individuals. Examples include:

» Helping an elderly relative;
» Saying kind words to everyone;
» Smiling at everyone;
» Helping parents around the house;
» Taking care of younger siblings;
» Sharing toys and books with other children who come to play.

You could make a brightly coloured money box with a slot at the top. Get your child to put your small change into the box. When it is full you can give it to charity and explain to them where the money is going with maps and pictures about less fortunate children. Encourage them to name blessings that they may take for granted that other children may not have. (A good tip for us adults, too!)

✏ OTHER ISLAMIC ACTS

As Islam is a complete way of life, there are numerous little actions that you can make part of your everyday life that are a *sunnah*, such as:

» Saying *bismillah* out loud before you start a meal and *alhamdulillah* once you have finished;
» Eating with your right hand;
» Using the daily *du'as* for sneezing, getting dressed etc.;
» Always using Islamic words in everyday conversation such as *insha'Allah*, *masha'Allah*, *subhanAllah*;
» Saying please and thank you or *jazakAllah* to everyone;
» Always greeting all Muslims with *as salaam alaikum* and asking your child to greet others in the same way.

These simple but blessed acts will soon become second nature for you and, by extension, for your child. They will be reminded of Allah throughout the day and, insha'Allah, be grateful for whatever He has provided.

✏ MUSIC AND TV

Islam does not allow musical instruments, the sound of musical instruments and singing that accompanies musical instruments. Thus the truly Islamic home should be free of music as this is of no benefit and is in fact detrimental to the heart of a believer.

Songs make hypocrisy grow in the heart just as water makes crops grow. (Al-Bayhaqi, Shu'ab al-Iman)

It is permissible to listen to the praise of Allah or other such purely religious matter 'sung' by a male voice in a sober manner without the use of instruments. Such 'songs' are known as *nasheeds* and there is no harm in listening to these on special occasions such as Eid. However, you need to be careful that a number of *nasheeds* on the market nowadays resemble pop/rap songs and use or try to imitate the sound of musical instruments and this is just as *haram*.

A number of children's items also come with an in-built musical facility such baby swings, walkers and even potties! If it is possible to purchase a non-musical alternative then it is preferable to do so, otherwise you can disable the musical facility.

There are few benefits to be had from TV, so it is better to limit the time spent watching it. In any case, your child will learn far more from active play and social interaction than from passively sitting in front of a screen. Insha'Allah, the whole family will benefit from the peace and quiet of not having the background noise of music or TV on all the time. Having said that, there will be times when you may need to occupy your children or when they do request to watch something. You can exercise more control over what they watch by buying Islamic children's DVDs, for example. However, do bear in mind that this is no substitute for spending quality time with your child.

✏ IMAGES

The use of images in Islam is not permitted as Abu Talhah, 'Ali and others ⁂ reported that Allah's Messenger ﷺ said:

> "Indeed, the angels do not enter a house in which there is a dog or an image (picture)." (Bukhari and Muslim)

This means that the Islamic home should be free of images of human and animal forms everywhere including the display of photographs, wall hangings, decorative pieces, furnishings and the like.

It is almost impossible to avoid images in books and other educational resources, but if you are going to use them solely for the purpose of education and development then they are permitted. However, do make sure that you put them away out of sight after your child has finished with them.

It is not necessary, however, to have figures and children's characters on bed linen, curtains, clothing, cups and plates etc. as this is not educational or fun and there are plenty of plain alternatives that can be used. The key is to strike a balance between providing fun and joy to a child in their play and education but at the same time ensuring that we respect the commands of Allah.

✏ OUTSIDE THE HOME

You may feel at times, that despite all your best efforts to provide an Islamic environment, it is not having the desired effect on your child. It may be worth looking further afield to see what influences your child is exposed to outside the home. Children very quickly pick up not-so-desirable habits from other children, even extended family members. For example, they may go to a home where music is considered acceptable or where films and cartoons are always on TV. Of course, they will find this novel and appealing and ask you if they can have the same at home as well.

It is important not to dismiss their request outright but to sit with them and spend time explaining in an age-appropriate and calm manner why this is not possible. Always try to offer an Islamically permissible alternative so your child does not feel deprived and left-out.

IN SHORT:

- Ensure that salah is established within the home.

- Make the Qur'an a part of daily life.

- Encourage each other to do acts of sadaqah.

- Try to incorporate as many sunan as possible into everyday life.

- Take a look around your house and remove those things that do not have a place in an Islamic home.

CHAPTER THREE

CREATING A CHILD FRIENDLY HOME

Once the home is set up in an Islamic way, there are just a few more steps that are needed to create a home that is happy and focused on the needs of the child.

➥ FAMILY LIFE

Parents set the tone for the atmosphere within the home, both in the way that they behave as individuals and their relationship with each other. This has a direct impact on how their children behave and form relationships. A home in which the husband and wife often have disagreements will only encourage children to be argumentative and disrespectful. If your child sees that you both spend a great deal of time watching TV, talking on your mobiles or working on your computers rather than communicating with each other, then that is what they will be drawn towards. On the other hand, if you both speak respectfully and kindly to each other and your child, focus on doing good deeds and positive actions as a family unit, then you will see that your child will automatically behave in the same way.

It is equally important for children to be respectful towards their siblings:

> The right of an elder brother over the younger ones is like the right of the father over his children.
> (Al-Bayhaqi, Shu'ab al-Iman)

Younger siblings should be encouraged to speak and treat their elder siblings with respect in return for enjoying the care and protection of older siblings. This fosters unity and closeness within the family, a sense of caring for and looking after each other's needs rather than the greedy, selfish individual centred people that we so often see around us today.

A good Muslim should be a hospitable host and meet with other members of the community as this maintains good relations. However, it is important to take care of the needs of your child as well in this respect. Avoid the temptation to drag your child to endless social functions or always having guests around, especially late in the evenings as this will disrupt their routine. Children thrive on routines and schedule, so it is important to have a loose timetable in place for eating and sleeping. When children know what to expect and when to expect it, they feel more secure and are less likely to act up.

If you do go out or have people around, ensure that your child's needs are met, by feeding them at their mealtimes, allowing them to sleep when it is time to do so and giving them activities to keep them occupied. In this way, they do not feel neglected and resort to bad behaviour for attention and you can enjoy your function.

✏ PRESENTATION OF THE HOME

You must not underestimate the impact of your home's presentation on your child's well-being. A great deal of thought goes into the presentation of nursery and school classrooms ensuring that they are light, spacious, clean, attractive and safe spaces that encourage learning. You can bring the same principles into your house.

Firstly, the home must be made safe for your child and it is really worth spending some time over this. Make sure that the appropriate stairgates and guards are in place as well as drawer locks, corner protectors, socket guards etc. Not only will this keep your child safe but it will also prevent you having to constantly tell your child off for exploring where they shouldn't!

Secondly, remove anything in the home that is forbidden in Islam such as images and music and the like (see previous chapter). There are a number of beautiful artworks that can be displayed in the home such as sceneries and Islamic calligraphy. In your child's room you can put up colourful alphabets, *du'as* and calendars, for example.

You don't have to fill your house with the most expensive furniture and decorative items for it to be home. By keeping it simple, your child will realise that a home is made with love, faith and respect and not material items. In any case, the fewer things you have, the less cluttered the space and the easier it is for you to clean. The less furniture there is, the more space there is for play or prayer. In fact it is a *sunnah* to sit on the floor. This is a great opportunity to generally think about the number of things that you and your family actually need.

If possible try to keep your child's play room and bedroom separate so that their bedroom is just the place where they sleep and possibly pray. Children do not need a lot of toys, but whatever you do provide them, make sure they are put away in labelled boxes. When they would like to play with them, they can get them easily and then put them away. This will encourage tidiness and organisation. Also make sure that they have easy access to age-appropriate books and writing paper and pens at all times. Even scrap paper should be kept and used. Plastic bottles and cardboard boxes that you would otherwise throw out can be put to use for creative activities.

Islam encourages parents to provide for their children, if it promotes good and to shelter them from poverty. This action is considered as charity and carries a reward, insha'Allah. Abu Mas'ood al-Badri ﷺ said:

> "The Prophet ﷺ said: 'When a man spends on his family with the intention of pleasing Allah, then it will be counted as sadaqah (charity) on his part.'"
> (Bukhari and Muslim)

➯ RULES

Rules provide the basis for a stable and secure child to move seamlessly into the world as rule systems are in place everywhere in society as well as in Islam. A home rule system is an effective way to draw attention to what your child is allowed to do and what they are not allowed to do. Many rules will be governed by Islam, others by your personal preference for how you would like your child to act. You may put whatever you feel is necessary to the plan. An example would be:

Rules in the Khan Household

1. Sit down when drinking and eating
2. Remember to say Bismillah before starting to eat
3. Remember to say Alhamdulillah after finishing a meal
4. No jumping on the furniture
5. Put everything away after play
6. Wash hands after going to the bathroom
7. Only enter mum and dad's room with permission
8. Share your toys
9. Please, no drawing on the wall
10. Respect all members of the family and no shouting at anyone

If you write out the rules with your child then they will feel more involved in the rule making process and more likely to comply. Even if your child is too young to read, it is still worth setting out the rules in this way. Both you and the child will be working from the same reference point and it helps everyone to be fair if you can show them which rule they have broken. To this end, the rules need to be placed somewhere where they can easily be seen and referred to such as on the fridge door.

In short:

☞ Treat your spouse and child with respect.

☞ Encourage your children to treat each other with respect and kindness.

☞ Meet the physical and emotional needs of your child.

☞ Provide safe, clean areas for your child to play and sleep in.

☞ Set boundaries (in writing) for your child to be adhered to.

CHAPTER FOUR

RAISING HEALTHY CHILDREN

The health and diet of your child will affect their performance as individuals. Certain foods can cause hyperactivity and aggression, while too much food and not enough activity will lead to laziness and obesity. Eating habits are learned very young, so if you can make healthy lifestyle choices for your child, they are much more likely to do the same for themselves as an adult.

✏ FOOD

O ye people! Eat of what is on earth, lawful (*halal*) and good (*tayyib*)... (Surah al-Baqarah 2:168)

The first point regarding food is that it must be *halal*, in that the meat is slaughtered according to Islamic Law and that the food is purchased with income that is earned in a *halal* manner. The second issue is that of *tayyib* which means pure, wholesome, clean and good. When you shop for food, do make sure that you check ingredients labels thoroughly, not just for whether a food is legally *halal* but also for the artificial colours, sweeteners and flavours that can be added to food. Some of these can be detrimental to children's health. Try to make meals at home from fresh, wholesome ingredients. This way you know what is going into your body and it will probably work out cheaper as well.

You need to understand the dietary needs of your child for their age and this may not necessarily match the needs of the rest of the family. For example, babies and toddlers benefit from whole fat foods in their diet but no added salt and sugar. If you introduce a variety of vegetables and fruits from an early age, they will develop a taste for these rather than foods that may not be so healthy. Every child has times that they are fussy about eating, so here are a few tips to help get your little one to eat:

» Present food attractively on the plate. For example, slices of round carrots and sticks of cucumber can be arranged as a flower.

» Children are more likely to eat if they are with other children who are eating.

» If, for example, you have a child who will not eat their greens, have a little tasting session with them. Cut up a variety of green vegetables (cooked and uncooked) and arrange them on a plate, such as broccoli, peas, green pepper, cucumber etc. Both of you can taste each vegetable and talk about the different tastes, textures and shapes. Explain the benefits of eating well in terms that they can understand. For instance, "If you want to play football well, then eating these foods will help you be strong and healthy." You can, of course, do this with different foods and drinks.

» If your child still does not want to eat a particular item, then do not get angry or force the issue. Just leave it and try again at a later stage.

» A final point is not to use food and especially sweets, as treats for good behaviour or withhold them as punishment.

Other Islamic etiquettes that you can introduce:

» Teach your child to say *bismillah* before starting to eat and *alhamdulillah* when they have finished.

» Make sure that, whenever possible, meals are eaten together as a family. This is a great way to spend quality time together.

» Let them have a go in serving themselves or if everyone is eating from one plate (which is *sunnah*) let them help you serve.

» Teach children to put a small amount on their plate. If they still need more then they can have seconds. This prevents wastage of food and drink that must be discouraged. To this end, do the same yourself, and freeze or refrigerate the leftovers instead of throwing anything away.

➥ PHYSICAL ACTIVITY

Children naturally have a lot of energy and are very physically active. This is something that needs to be encouraged and there are several benefits to this. Children who exercise regularly:

» Develop stronger muscles and bones;
» Are less likely to be overweight;
» Have a decreased risk of future diseases such as Coronary Artery Disease and Type II diabetes;
» Sleep better;
» May have better skills such as hand-eye co-ordination, teamwork and other benefits that arise from playing sports;
» Get rid of their excess energy and are therefore less likely to behave in a destructive manner.

Try to incorporate some sort of activity every day or at least as regularly as possible for a minimum of an hour a day. This can be broken up into smaller time slots, so you may wish to have a bout of activity in the morning when your child is fresh and energetic and again in the late afternoon or evening to tire them out before they have a bath and go to sleep. Simple examples are:

» Simply kicking a ball (this can be done indoors as well with a soft ball);
» Playing with a bat and ball will help with hand-eye co-ordination;
» Playing hide and seek in the house (make sure children can't lock themselves into rooms);
» Flying a kite (especially one that they have made themselves);
» Blowing bubbles and running after them;
» Using a skipping rope;

» Race with you or each other;
» Obstacle course;
» Walking or cycling/scooter.

If you have access to an outside space such as your own garden or a nearby park, try to get out as much as possible, even if the weather is not ideal. Providing that your child is ideally dressed, they do not mind if it is drizzling or cloudy.

If that is not possible, then there are simple exercise routines that can be done at home. You can make these up yourself with your child to involve and motivate them. The following routine, for example, incorporates endurance, strength and flexibility.

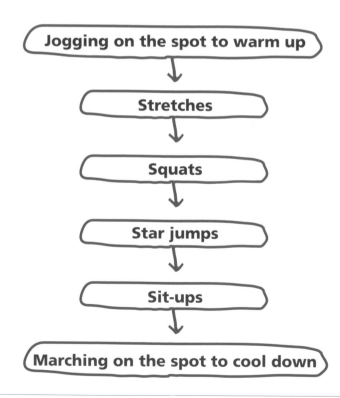

✏ BATHING

Islam attaches great importance to hygiene and physical cleanliness. Indeed it is reported from Abu Malik al-Ash'ari that the Messenger of Allah ﷺ said:

"Cleanliness is half of faith..." (Muslim)

Performing *ghusl* is in fact an Islamic teaching that the Prophet ﷺ passed on as being an obligatory practice. Narrated Abu Sa'id al-Khudri ﷺ that the Messenger of Allah ﷺ said:

"The taking of a bath on Friday is compulsory for every Muslim who has attained the age of puberty." (Bukhari)

Babies and young toddlers usually love bathing and playing in water. However, older children may be more resistant to having a bath as they may be involved in play or know that a bath signals bedtime. If you put a little effort into making bath time fun and enjoyable for your child, then they will look forward to bathing regularly and keeping clean. The following ideas may help:

» Bring play items into the bath such as bath toys and books.
» Get some bubble bath. Let your child pour it in and watch the bubbles form.
» Allocate a special wash cloth or sponge that they use to clean themselves with.

If possible, try to fulfil the *sunnah* of bathing your child on a Friday, while explaining the importance of this day. After the bath, you can dress your child in their best clothes, so they feel that it is a special day. It is after all the most superior and blessed of days and a routine like this will instil a sense of this early on.

➥ TEETH

As soon as your baby grows their first tooth, you can start brushing. At first, you will need to show them how to do this most effectively. As they grow older and start to want more independence, then toddlers will want to brush their own teeth. Allow them to do this. If your child is not so conscientious about cleaning their teeth then the following tips should help:

» Explain the importance of brushing their teeth;
» Allow them to pick their own toothbrush;
» Let them choose a toothpaste;
» Motivate them, for example, "Masha'Allah, Safiyyah, you have your own pink toothbrush. Are you going to show me how you brush your teeth?";
» Always praise your child when they brush their teeth;
» If you have more than one child, they can brush their teeth together as children like to imitate others;
» Be a role model and brush your teeth in front of them as well.

It is recommended practice to use a *siwaak* (*miswak*) as this was the practice of the Prophet ﷺ. He said:

> *"If it were not for the fact that I did not want to overburden my ummah, I would have ordered them to use siwaak before every prayer."* (Muslim)

This is a great opportunity to use a *siwaak* yourself and introduce the idea to your child.

Safiyyah's Toothbrush

✏ HAIR

The Prophet ﷺ did not like people to leave their hair unkempt and dirty and it is a *sunnah* of the Prophet ﷺ to look after the hair. He ﷺ said:

> *"Whoever has hair, let him look after it properly."*
> (Abu Dawud)

It is important therefore to take care of the hair and consider it a blessing of Allah, while respecting it. This means that it is unnecessary to make dramatic statements about appearance through the hair and styling it in unnatural ways. You can encourage your child to take care of their hair by:

» Letting them choose a comb or brush, which is their own special one;
» Let them have a go at washing and brushing their hair;
» Talk about the importance of washing and looking after their hair;
» When they have washed and brushed their hair praise them, tell them how nice they look, masha'Allah;
» Brush your hair in front of them, as they will imitate you.

✏ TOILET TRAINING

There is a large amount of guidance regarding potty training, the best time to start and the various methods of doing so. This will be different for each child, parent and circumstances. But there are a few things to bear in mind from an Islamic point of view:

» Always wash your child rather than wipe them with tissues or wet wipes. Wash them with your left hand and teach them to do the same.

» Spread waterproof sheets down in the house in case of accidents. These can be taken up and washed without compromising the cleanliness of the room that you may use to pray in. Anything that gets a toddler's urine on it must be washed.

» Encourage and praise your child's efforts but never get angry if they don't always get it right.

» Explain the concept and importance of *taharah*.

» Boys should be taught to urinate sitting down as this is the *sunnah* and will be less messy as well.

» Your child should always wash their hands after they have been to the toilet. You can encourage this by getting a step that they can use to reach the basin and their special soap and towel.

➯ wudu

As an extension to praying in the presence of your child in order to teach them *salah*, it is also worth doing your *wudu* in front of them thoroughly and correctly. The benefits of *wudu* are numerous. It cleanses the body as well as the soul and erases sins. The Prophet ﷺ said:

> *"The key to Paradise is salah and the key to salah is wudu."* (At-Tirmidhi)

Soon your child will start to copy you and you can talk them through the *wudu*, by asking them to wash their hands three times etc. You do not need to do this every prayer time, but maybe in the mornings, so that *wudu* becomes part of their nature just like brushing their teeth. By the time *salah* becomes obligatory on them, they will already have learnt their *wudu*, insha'Allah.

IN SHORT:

- Ensure that the diet of the whole family is halal and tayyib as prescribed in the Qur'an.

- Allow plenty of time and opportunity for physical exercise and sport, outside if possible.

- Make bath times fun and enjoyable.

- Look after your baby's teeth and hair and encourage toddlers to do this for themselves.

- Get your child into the habit of doing wudu.

CHAPTER FIVE

HOW TO DEAL WITH A DISRUPTIVE CHILD

Most parents will experience disruptive behaviour on the part of their child at some point during their lives and this is to be considered a normal part of growing up. Almost all children like to do the opposite of what they are told as their minds are still exploring the world around them. However, whether or not that behaviour continues will depend on how you first handle the situation. If your child is disruptive only for a short period of time, it may just be because of a simple reason such as hunger or tiredness. If your child has been behaving this way for some time, it can be very draining on both parents and it is easy to feel that there is no hope. However, all phases of a child's life are temporary and will pass, insha'Allah.

Your duty as a parent is to nurture your child towards the right direction rather than just leave them to their own devices. Sometimes children can start being disruptive because they have no rules or it is not clear to them where their boundaries are. Do set rules, do show them who is in charge and do show them that you love them by talking to them and being patient with them. Remember that discipline is an important aspect of bringing up your child as the Prophet ﷺ said:

"*I have only been sent to make righteous behaviour complete.*" (Bukhari)

Other reasons why children may start to become disruptive include:

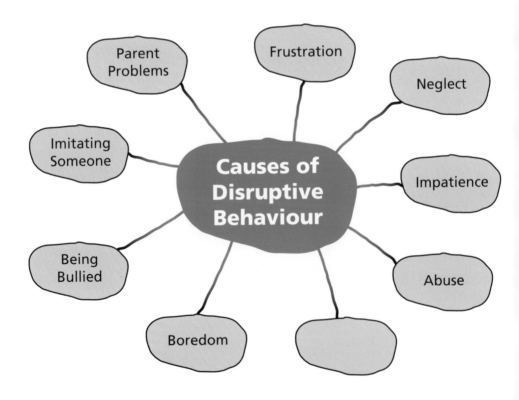

As there are different causes for disruptive behaviour, there are also different ways of dealing with it. You need to step back and spend some time observing why this behaviour develops in the first place and then look at the best way to help your child. It is most effective if both parents work with each other to sort out any issues.

✏ ADDRESS YOUR CHILD BY THEIR NAME

This simple *sunnah* of treating people, including your child, with gentleness and respect will almost always save you from having to counteract bad behaviour. Try to use words of endearment when addressing your child, such as "my darling" or "dear". This will discourage them from doing anything that they are not supposed to do. Not only will they learn these words of affection, they will become more respectful towards you. There are many examples of prophets addressing their children with words of endearment. For example, Prophet Yaqub ﷺ cautioned his sons as follows:

> **O my beloved sons! Enter not all by one gate; enter ye by different gates.** (Surah Yusuf 12:67)

If your child still does not respond to you, then address them using their full name but maintaining a calm and clear manner. Continue to use an increasingly authoritative and firm tone of voice but do remember not to shout. Shouting will only teach children to shout back to you and others, resulting in a demanding personality that is insensitive to the needs of others.

✏ SPEND TIME WITH & TALK TO YOUR CHILD

It is essential to spend quality time with your child, playing and talking with them. Not only is it fun for you both, it helps foster a good relationship between you and makes the child feel valued. It is all too easy to neglect a child's emotional and spiritual needs especially in a large family. It goes without saying that it is hard to spend time individually with each child if you have other children, and even if you don't. However, a golden rule is for each parent to set aside at least half an hour for each child to spend as the child wishes. It would be no exaggeration to say that just this small amount of your time will pay dividends for your child's future life. They are much less likely to misbehave if they feel that they are being given your complete and undivided attention.

If despite benefitting from your undivided attention and calm manner, your child still behaves badly, it is tempting to just shout at them. Don't give into temptation! Hold your child, ask them what is wrong and what they are feeling. If they are too young to articulate themselves then ask them specific questions to find out how they feel. Reassure them that you want to work with them to sort out the problem. Once your child realises that you are on their side, then they will insha'Allah calm down.

For example, a common problem is that you tell your child you cannot buy them a particular toy in the shop. They respond by crying and acting out. What do you do? The best thing is to remain calm yourself. Stop whatever you are doing, address them by their name, hold their hand, get down to their level and with a firm but calm voice explain to them why they cannot have that toy in clear and simple language. Explain, for example, that they have plenty of toys at home and that you will, insha'Allah, take them to the park later to play on the swings. You must, however, never promise to give a reward to a child that you do not intend to give them as this counts as a lie and your child will lose their trust in you. When you have the time, you may consider telling your children, in an age-appropriate manner, about those less fortunate than themselves who do not even have enough food or clean water.

➡ TIME OUT

Toddler tantrums are exhausting and embarrassing for parents. It takes quiet and determined effort to calm your child down without getting agitated yourself. There are stages in your child's life when they are more prone to tantrums (think "terrible twos"!) but even older children can respond to certain triggers by screaming, shouting and hitting out.

Again, the first thing to do is to remain calm yourself and start by talking to your child as above. If you find that this is not working even though you have made it clear what they have done wrong and why, then put them in the "time out spot". This is a clean and safe area of the house such as a corner or a step (but never a cupboard) that you always use for this purpose. While doing this, you must be gentle but firm and do not show your anger. If your child moves from their spot, then simply pick them up and put them back, all the while explaining why you are doing this. Ask them to think about what they have done wrong and use the quiet time to calm down. This may take a while, but it does work. However, you and your spouse (or other carers) must be consistent in implementing the time-out for it to be most effective.

The Prophet Muhammad ﷺ responded to lying by ignoring the liar as the following *hadith* indicates:

> *If the Messenger of Allah came to know that one of his household told a lie, he would try and ignore him until he repented.* (Ahmad)

It is interesting to note that he did not become angry, so neither should you when confronted by less than Islamic behaviour. If the child is too young to understand your silence then explain it to them in the context of the *hadith*. Insha'Allah they will recognise the enormity of their actions, apologise and not repeat it.

✏ REWARD CHARTS

Your patience can be tested if your child refuses to do the little tasks that you ask of them, such as tidy their room. Instead of punishing the bad behaviour, it can sometimes be easier to encourage the good behaviour instead.

Every time your child does something that you have asked, reward them with a star sticker or stamp (or anything that represents achievement) on a brightly-coloured reward chart placed prominently in the house. You may wish to reward them with a gift or treat if they can accumulate a certain number of rewards within a certain amount of time. Again remember to only promise them what you can actually fulfil as the following *hadith* narrated by Abdullah ibn Amir ﷺ cautions:

> *"My mother called me one day when Allah's Messenger ﷺ was in our house. She said, 'Come and I will give you something.' Allah's Messenger ﷺ asked her, 'What do*

you intend to give him?' She said, 'I want to give him dates.' The Prophet ﷺ said, 'If you were not to give him something, your statement would be recorded against you as a lie.'" (Abu Dawud)

If you set out targets that your child should achieve, then the reward chart technique will instil a sense of achieving goals. In addition, your child will realise that if they work steadily and patiently then they will be rewarded for it, which is a good habit to set up for life and a good basis to explain the life of this world and the reward in the next.

✎ TEN DOs BEHAVIOUR ACTION PLAN

1 DO establish ground rules.
2 DO involve your child in these rules.
3 DO make rules positive and fair.
4 DO remind your child what Islam says about respecting parents.
5 DO praise your child.
6 DO give them activities to keep them stimulated.
7 DO introduce new activities.
8 DO encourage your child to do good and forbid evil.
9 DO reward your child.
10 DO give time to your child.

Of course there are many other things that should be done but these are some to focus on.

By implementing these suggestions regularly and consistently, you will insha'Allah find that a disruptive child will become a much more pleasant little person to be around and that, in turn you and other members of the family will be much more relaxed. These suggestions can also be used for a child that is not disruptive and you will find that you rarely have to caution them for bad behaviour.

CHAPTER SIX

INTELLECTUAL DEVELOPMENT AND PLAY

Play is a major part of every baby and toddler's learning process. On the face of it, it may seem to be a meaningless set of activities to just pass the time until they go to school, but it is through these activities that your child will develop their intellectual function.

During the first year your baby will be observing objects and people. As they get older they will learn to explore these things in more detail. Before you know it, your child will be crawling, shuffling or walking towards these objects and examining them in depth, using their mouths and hands. This is all helping them to develop an understanding of the world around them as well as their thought process, memory, attention and other functions of the brain.

✎ THE IMPORTANCE OF THE QUR'AN IN INTELLECTUAL DEVELOPMENT

The brain is obviously an organ of intellectual capacity, but Islam also places great emphasis on the heart as an organ of understanding.

> **...their hearts are sealed, and so they understand not.** (Surah at-Tawba 9:87)

> **But only he (will prosper) that brings to Allah a sound heart (*qalb saleem*).** (Surah ash-Shu'ara 26:89)

Thus, any programme of intellectual development for your child must not only focus on developing their brain functions but also a sound heart at the same time. The heart is the core of a believer and affects everything that a believer does, thus developing your child's heart (and yours at the same time) will be of the greatest benefit in this life and the next. The best way to feed the whole intellect of your child, brain and heart, is to introduce the Qur'an to them from the earliest age on a regular basis. There is within the Qur'an everything that a child needs to think about science, history, mathematics, language, the opportunity to develop their memory as well as providing comfort to the heart.

(Here is) a book which we have sent down unto thee, full of blessings, that they may meditate on its signs, and that men of understanding may receive admonition. (Surah Sad 38:29)

For without doubt in the remembrance of Allah do hearts find satisfaction. (Surah ar-Rad 13:28)

You can refer back to the Qur'an section in Chapter Two for how best to incorporate Qur'an in your child's life and remember that it is never too early to start.

➡ MEMORY AND THOUGHT

The Companions of the Prophet had excellent memories. They committed the Qur'an and many thousands of *ahadith* to memory. Nowadays we seem to have much less of a capacity to store information in our minds and we rely more on books and computers. It is worth cultivating the capacity for memory in your child. The more that you encourage them to learn at an early age, the more they will remember. As Ibn Qayyim al-Jawziyya explains in his book, *Medicine of the Prophet*:

"Any limb which has much exercise becomes strong, and especially according to the type of that exercise. Rather is that the case with every faculty, for if a man concentrates much on learning by heart his memory is strengthened, and if he thinks a good deal, his cognitive (mental) faculty is strengthened."

Another good quality to nurture is the faculty of thought. Allah frequently calls upon the '*Ulul albab*' (men of understanding) to think and reflect upon his signs.

The best way to progress memory and the ability to reflect is simply to recite and memorise the Qur'an. Committing as much of the Qur'an as possible to memory will help improve the memory function in general and there is a great deal in the Qur'an upon which a person of any age can reflect.

➩ SENSORY EXPERIENCES

Our five senses are touch, smell, sight, hearing and taste. Babies and young children are constantly surrounded by sensory experiences, all of which are new and exciting for them. To help develop and stimulate your baby's senses here are some things you can do:

Hearing	Sight
» Listen to the Qur'an on audio	» Hang mobiles e.g. in the cot
» Recite the Qur'an to them yourself	» Place brightly coloured objects around them
» Talk to them using varying tones of voice	» Hang coloured lights for them to stare at
» Read to them with expression	» Let them look at pictures in baby books

Taste and Smell	Touch
» Milk and water, if needed	» Let them feel soft 'feely' books
» Smooth purees of one type of food e.g. mashed banana	» Let them handle a treasure bag - a bag full of different objects with different textures
» Textured food e.g. cereal	
» Mixture of food e.g. chicken, broccoli and potato	» Play with sensory toys
» Warm food as well as chilled food such as yogurt	» Place them on different surfaces to play e.g. rug, duvet, carpet, grass

As your child gets older their sensory experiences become more sophisticated, thus the play you provide can be more complex and activities can now take place outdoors as well as indoors:

Hearing	Sight
» Introduce different languages and speech	» Introduce shapes and colour and spot where they appear e.g. round green apple, triangular red roof
» Listen to different readings of the Qur'an	
» Compare loud and soft noises	» Play observation games such as 'I Spy' and 'Spot the difference'
» Listen to animal noises e.g. rainforest audio tracks	
» Listen out for everyday sounds e.g. bird song, fire engine, lawn mower, leaves rustling	» Look at the shape of Arabic writing and numbers

Hearing	Sight
» Introduce more complex flavours	» Feel different textures e.g. fabric, rice, wood etc
» Smell things e.g. coffee, lemon, soap, flowers	» Make a feely bag/basket and name the textures e.g. soft, hard, smooth, rough
» Discuss favourite smells and tastes	» Allow them to touch grass, leaves, trees in the garden
» Cook with them or let them help you cook	» Touch things with elbows and knees as well as hands
	» Touch cool and warm things

✏ AGE APPROPRIATE ACTIVITIES

Allowing your child to play in an age appropriate manner will help develop their attention and memory and keep them stimulated. Babies love watching other people, so they will respond positively to being spoken to and sung to with plenty of actions and expression. You will love hearing them giggle as you play simple games such as 'peek-a-boo'. Once they become mobile and start to crawl, they will want to investigate what you have in your hand, and also, unfortunately, what is in your drawers. It will help if you can keep a selection of everyday items to hand, so that your baby can explore these without pulling the house apart!

Toddlers are able to play alone for a while; they repeat actions and learn through trial and error. However, you do not need to buy them an expensive array of toys to keep them stimulated. A toddler will be just as happy with a plastic spoon and plastic box, banging the two and discovering the sound they make. They will also enjoy building bricks that they can stack, small boxes that they can put things in and take out of, and large crayons and scrap paper that they can scribble on.

Toddlers also love imitating adults and will be thrilled if you involve them in your everyday activities. You can ask them to help you put clothes in the laundry basket, for example, or give them play gardening tools which they help mum and dad with in the garden. They will feel like a valued member of the household and understand the value of teamwork and doing their bit. They will ask you questions about what you are doing, 'How does this work?', 'What is this for?' and that dreaded question 'Why?' Answer them patiently and as best you can and you will help nurture their naturally inquisitive minds. If you don't know the answer then you could go to the library together to find out and you will have learnt something yourself in the process.

Most everyday items and activities can be made interesting for a toddler, no matter how mundane they may seem. Your child is seeing the world through fresh eyes, so exposing them to new experiences in a controlled and safe way at this stage will keep them open to new experiences in their future lives, insha'Allah.

✏ THINGS TO MAKE AND DO AT HOME

Here are ideas of things you can make and do from everyday items in the house:

Light: Babies are especially attracted to light. Simply draw the curtains and move a torch around the room and you will notice how your baby is fascinated by the moving light. You can stick different coloured tissue paper in front of the torch for different effects.

Bottles: Thoroughly wash out an empty transparent plastic bottle. You can part fill it with water and food colouring or glitter. Ensure that the lid is tightly sealed by taping it up. Little children will have fun watching the coloured water or glitter as well as listening to the sound of the liquid.

Mobile: You can make a baby mobile with a number of objects, such as small, light toys, soft books, kitchen roll tubes or cotton reels. String these objects up with a short length of string to a rod or stick. Hang it safely just within reach of your child where they can 'bat' at it and watch their delighted expressions.

Kitchen tools: If you are working in the kitchen, there are a number of things that you can give your child to play with. Do ensure that any items you give your child are clean and not sharp or broken. Babies love to put new objects in their mouth so make it baby safe. Your baby will be quite happy with a plastic spoon and plastic cup to bang together. Older children will love to pretend they are cooking if they are provided with small, plastic kitchen items.

Feely bag, basket or box: This is a simple way for your baby to develop their sense of touch and explore new items. For example, you could put the following things in the bag: a comb, toothbrush, shell, straw, cotton wool, acorn etc. Your child then reaches in and holds one object in their hand. Without taking it out of the bag and looking at it, they can describe to you how it feels and what they think it is. Then they can take it out of the bag and see if they are right. This is also good for increasing their descriptive vocabulary.

Boxes: Big cardboard boxes have many uses and if you do happen to have any in the house, let your child play with them. Younger children will get pleasure from simply putting things in and taking things out of the box. They can even climb in themselves if it is big enough, although you must ensure that they cannot close themselves in. Older children will have fun painting and decorating a box that they can use to put their toys in.

Junk Modelling: There are endless possibilities with small boxes, yogurt pots, straws, scrap paper and other things that you would only think of throwing out. These can be put together in various combinations to create models of cars, houses or aeroplanes among other things. Not only will children find this great fun, it is also good practice for them in learning how to plan and construct something. The model can be painted and decorated to make it look nice. Once your child has finished making it, do give the finished piece pride of place in the house so that they feel a sense of achievement.

Posters: A fun way to allow your child to express themselves is through painting and drawing. Make sure that they have a variety of coloured pencils, felt tip pens, crayons and paints so that they can explore the different effects of each of these. Give them a large sheet of paper and allow their imaginations to run wild in producing a piece of artwork and ask them to talk about they are drawing. Alternatively, you can give them some direction and help them make a poster for their bedroom with, for example, a *du'a* on it or a landscape. You can help them experiment with different techniques such as smudging colours together or dabbing on paint with a sponge.

Thread and bead: This activity is very effective for instilling patience and developing hand-eye co-ordination in children. For this you will need empty cotton reels or buttons with holes in them as well as string, shoe lace or some other connector. The aim is for your child to thread the string through a certain number of cotton reels or buttons. You can make this into a competition to see how fast they can do it and you will see that with practice they get better.

Sand: If you can provide your child with sand in a bucket, they are sure to have lots of fun. Not only can they make little sandcastles, but you can also teach them about the different textures and properties of wet and dry sand, for example.

Kim's game: This game is really good for developing memory. You will need to collect about five everyday items from around the house and put them on a table or a tray. Go through the items you have with your child and give them a few moments to memorise what is there. Cover the items with a cloth and, without letting your child see, take one item away. Remove the cloth and ask your child to name the missing item. As your child gets better at this, you can add more items to the tray.

IN SHORT:

- ➢ Expose your child to a variety of different experiences for each of their senses.

- ➢ Use everyday household items creatively to provide play opportunities for your child.

- ➢ Make sure that the Qur'an is part of their lives in order to develop their hearts as well.

- ➢ Ensure that all activities are age appropriate so that your child will get the most out of their activities.

CHAPTER SEVEN

CHILD DEVELOPMENT

As your child gets older, it is important to concentrate on developing specific skills in order to help them become balanced individuals in later life. However, do remember that they are still children and that these skills can be learnt through play and taught in a fun manner and will have a greater impact than if taught by rote. The following skills are in the foundation stage of the early learning curriculum.

Communication, Language and Literacy

This includes language for communication; language for thinking; linking sounds and letters; reading; writing; handwriting.

Problem Solving, Reasoning and Numeracy

This includes numbers as labels and for counting; calculating; shape, space and measures.

Knowledge and Understanding of the World

This includes exploration and investigation, designing and making; ICT (Information and communications technology); time; place; communities.

Creative Development

This includes being creative – responding to experiences, expressing and communicating ideas; exploring media and materials; developing imagination and imaginative play.[1]

Physical Development

This includes movement and space; health and bodily awareness; using equipment and materials.

Personal, Social and Emotional Development

This includes dispositions and attitudes; self-confidence and self esteem; making relationships; behaviour and self-control; self-care; sense of community.

In addition, a Muslim child's curriculum should always include learning about Islam.

---

1   This part of the curriculum also includes creating music and dance. However, this has not been included as it is inappropriate within an Islamic environment.

This chapter provides ideas and suggestions to develop each of these key skills for the 3-5 year age group. You can mix and match the activities, make them more complex or simplify them according to the needs of your particular child. There are a wealth of resources that you can use and adapt to your own particular situation, keeping in mind your child's age, progress and interests.

☞ COMMUNICATION, LANGUAGE AND LITERACY

The best way for your child to learn language is by hearing you speak. So talk to your child...about anything. If you are in the kitchen, talk them through what are you are doing. Spend time talking to them about your interests or what you do at work. Encourage them to talk about what they like, what they are doing. Ask them simple questions to encourage them to respond. When your child speaks to you, listen and look at them with your full concentration. Do not interrupt your child while they are speaking. What they are saying is important. This will help ensure that when you speak, your child will extend you the same courtesy and learn the cycle of talking, listening and concentrating.

Read books, newspapers, magazines, food labels and cookery books in front of your children. Supply them with age appropriate books. They may not be able to read the words, but they will recognise the shapes of the letters and enjoy the pictures. With time they may start to link a particular sound with the shape of a letter and this forms the beginning, insha'Allah, of a lifelong love of reading.

The first revealed *ayat* of the Qur'an are very relevant here:

Read! And thy Lord is most bountiful. He Who taught (the use of) the pen. (Surah al-Qalam 96:3-4)

It will encourage children to read and write, if you explain to them that reading is a direct command from Allah and that it is the way they can gain knowledge and reward.

Other activities you can do at home:

Rhymes: Children will pick up catchy rhymes very quickly. So instead of teaching them meaningless nursery rhymes, make up some rhymes together that have an Islamic theme. For example:

I'm going to do my *salah*,
Then afterwards do my *du'a*,
Allah help me through my days,
To You is all worship and praise.

There are also a number of Islamic alternatives to the traditional nursery rhymes that you can find in books or on the internet.

Stories: Reading stories to children is a wonderful way to help develop their language skills, imagination and an understanding of the world around them. When you read, use a varied vocabulary and descriptive words to bring the pictures to life. Read with expression, point to the pictures and make actions. It will really help your child to enjoy the experience and engage with the story. Often your child will ask you to read the same book to them. This is fine and the repetition will help them to remember stories and words. But story telling does not have to be a passive activity on the child's part. You can relate the characters and events in the story to your own child's life. "Look at that little boy in the picture. He is going to the mosque with his daddy. You went to the mosque with your daddy on Friday. Do you remember?" You can also ask questions relating to the pictures. "What do you think that girl is saying to her sister?" Do be patient when waiting for an answer and praise your child when they express themselves.

Books: Build up a library of books for your child and put them on bookshelves where your child can easily access them to read and enjoy. The best books are Islamic books: books about the Prophet, the Companions, the Wives of the Prophet, notable male and female Muslims both past and present that can provide good role models. There are a growing number of Islamic story books and other books which have positive lessons and morals in them. Otherwise, you can adapt any book by giving the characters Muslim names and having them speak to each other using Islamic words such as *as salaam alaikum*, for example.

Draw and write: When you have told your child a particular story several times, ask them to draw a picture from the story and ask them to talk you through it and explain what they are drawing. If they are old enough to write then you can ask them to write anything from one word to a sentence to accompany their drawing as well. This will consolidate their knowledge and vocabulary. You can do this quite effectively with stories of the Prophets, for instance.

Posters: You can put up alphabet posters in your child's bedroom in the language that you would like them to learn. Your child will begin to recognise the shapes of the letters and the sequence they are in. You can also do this with words that you would like your child to learn, such as *insha'Allah*, *masha'Allah*. If you make these posters with your child, this will be even more effective.

Spellings: When your child is old enough to recognise letters and is beginning to write, then get them to practice reading and spelling Islamic words, such as the names of the prophets or simple words from the Qur'an.

➤ PROBLEM SOLVING, REASONING AND NUMERACY

This is not just about maths and doing sums on paper but includes counting, shapes, measures and numbers in all their forms. If you can make these concepts exciting and relevant to everyday activities then your child will be more likely to enjoy subjects such as maths later on in their academic life. Provide your child with toys such as jigsaw puzzles and pretend fruit and vegetable stalls that will help them with problem solving, shapes, patterns and counting out quantities and money. These are just a few of the activities to help get you started in this area:

Counting Games: Try to play numbers games with your child. For example, at home you could ask them to help you count out spoons to put on the dinner table for everyone in the family; when you are out driving in the car with your child or on the train, ask them to count how many of a certain object they can spot, such as red cars or buses. If you have more than one child you can make this into a competition.

Numbers: You can teach your child the importance of numbers in Islam. For example, the **5** pillars, the **5** daily prayers, the **6** articles of faith, the **3** divisions of *tawheed*, Surah al-Baqarah is the **2**nd chapter of the Qur'an, **2** *fard* in Fajr, **3** *fard* in Maghrib, **4** *fard* in Dhuhr and so on. As children get older, you can get them a small *tasbeeh* with 33 beads and encourage them to count out their *tasabeeh*, such *SubhanAllah*, *Alhamdulillah* and *Allahu Akbar*.

Shapes: Your child can draw or trace around different shapes. You can also get them to spot these shapes in everyday life, for example, an orange is round, an egg is oval. You can also compare the relative sizes of the same shapes, for example a water melon is the same shape as a blueberry but much bigger. This is a good way to keep them occupied while you are shopping.

Measure: While working in the kitchen, you can bring out the scales and visually explain the concept of light and heavy by getting them to hold different objects in their hands and then weighing them. For older children you can link this idea to the following *ayat*:

> **Then, he whose balance (of good deeds) will be (found) heavy, will be in a life of good pleasure and satisfaction. But he whose balance (of good deeds) will be (found) light, will have his home in a bottomless pit.**
> (Surah al-Qaria 101:6-9)

Insha'Allah, they will be able to be visualise the concept and importance of having a heavy scale of good deeds.

Sorting and ordering: Smaller children can play with shape sorting toys where they have to slot the correct shape in the correct hole. Older children can help you around the house and order their environment. For example, when they put away their toys, they can learn to stack them so that the smaller boxes are stacked on top of the bigger boxes and the bookshelf is organised according to the size of the books. They can also help you sort out the recycling boxes for instance, by putting the paper in one box and the plastics in another. In this way, they will also get a feel for how many things fit into a particular space.

Time: Learning to tell the time is a very useful skill to start early and it can be great fun. You can buy or make simple cardboard clock faces with movable hands and use these to teach your child how to tell the time. To link this in with the times for prayer, you can take 5 clock faces, label these Fajr through to 'Isha and set the time on each face to correspond with the *salah* time that day. You can put these clocks up on the wall so that the prayer timetable is much more visual. When the clock on the wall matches the clock of a particular prayer time, then your child can tell you what time it is and what prayer is due to be performed. Get your child to change the time on the prayer clocks daily by reading from a prayer timetable.

✏ KNOWLEDGE AND UNDERSTANDING OF THE WORLD

It is important that children have an understanding of what happens in the immediate surroundings that they live in as well as the wider world around them. This will make them, insha'Allah, into well-rounded individuals that care for the environment and all that is in it and appreciate the wonders of the world.

> **Behold! In the creation of the heavens and the earth and the alternation of night and day, there are indeed signs for men of understanding.** (Surah Ali Imran 3:190)

This also extends to being aware about other people. The more informed they are of the situation of others, the more grateful they will for the blessings they have and they will insha'Allah, be more tolerant and understanding of other people, beliefs and viewpoints. Explain the importance of getting along and understanding others. Let them know that the only reason that Allah made people different is so that they could get to know each other, share and learn from each other.

> **We created you from a single (pair) of a male and a female and made you into nations and tribes, that ye may know each other (not that ye may despise each other).** (Surah al-Hujurat 49:13)

Here are some ideas to get you started:

Observe outside: A very simple but important skill is to reflect and ponder over the creation of Allah. Sit with your child in the garden and observe. There is so much to see that it is worth concentrating on one area at a time and only go into the detail that is appropriate for your child's age. Observe the birds and how they fly. How do they use their wings, do they fly alone or together, randomly or in a pattern? Watch how they land, where do they land? Listen for the sound of birdsong. If you put a birdfeeder in your garden you can observe the eating habits of the birds. What different sizes and colours of birds can you see? You can do the same for different insects, animals, plants and trees at parks, the seaside or the local farm. If you repeat this activity every few weeks you will be amazed at how many changes take place over time and with the seasons.

Planting: It is most rewarding for children to see the fruits of their labour and one of the most exciting wonders of Allah's creation is planting a seemingly dead seed and watching it grow into a plant. In a small pot, plant a seed in a little soil (a sunflower is good). Leave it near a sunny window and get your child to be responsible for watering it every so often. You will see it germinates after a week and grows quite quickly after that. You can do the same with cress, which has the added advantage that your child will take great delight in eating it.

Outings: You can take your child to age-appropriate exhibitions and museums to discover more about the world as it is and as it was in the past both in this country and abroad. Expose your child to different surroundings and ask them to think about what they see and note the differences. For example, note the hustle and bustle of the local high street where there are houses, shops, places of worship, and cars, bikes and buses on the road. Compare this with a more rural setting where you can see more greenery and hear different sounds such as the singing of birds.

Jobs and Roles: Introduce your child to the different jobs and functions that people carry out and how important everyone's contribution is to society. Talk to them about the job that mummy or daddy does and what this involves. You can help your child draw uniforms and work places to symbolise different jobs. For example, a stethoscope and hospital can represent a doctor.

Maps and Globes: Maps are a great visual aid to explaining current affairs and history. You can help your child label the continents and major countries on a world map or globe. If you want to concentrate on a more detailed area, you could make a map of a particular country or region. For example, you could concentrate on the Middle East and show your child where Makkah and Madinah are and other important cities, such as Jerusalem.

Cultures: Explain to your child that although everyone eats and wears clothes, people from different cultures have different foods and clothes and speak different languages and dialects. Explore the different cultures by concentrating on one at a time, learning about their beliefs and customs. You can go to the library for books with pictures that your child can relate to. If you can, try to find recipes that you can cook or clothes that your child can wear. Your child will love learning how to say a word of greeting in a different language.

Mosques: It is really interesting to see the varying architecture of mosques around the world. These range from the simplest mud buildings to the most ornate and decorated places of worship. You can get pictures from the internet, books or Islamic calendars. Your child can have a go at copying the pictures and even designing their own mosque.

Trade: It is never too early to start to give your child some idea of the things that they use and may take for granted. You can look at the labels on food, clothes and toys to see where they come from and locate these countries on the world map. How did they arrive in this country? How did they get to the shops? How did you buy them? Your child will enjoy playing shopkeeper and selling you little goods which you can pay them for using made-up money.

➭ CREATIVE DEVELOPMENT

Creativity allows your child to express how they feel through the media of words, pictures and actions. By allowing your child to develop their creative side, you are allowing them to use their imagination and letting them make decisions about how they can express themselves using all their senses. It is important to let your child have some opportunity to express themselves freely, without telling them how they ought to do something. For example, if they want to construct a Lego house with the door on the roof, then let your child do so without telling them that that is wrong.

Drawing: Always let your child have easy access to pen and paper. The first way in which a child will express their creativity is by drawing. Little hands will benefit from big pens that are easy to hold and grip. Initially the drawings will appear to be random scribbles, but these will develop into meaningful patterns. Ask your child questions about what they have drawn to get a better idea what they are thinking about.

Pictures: Your child will have great fun painting pictures. They don't have to use a brush, they can use rags, sponges and even finger/hand/foot painting. To make them use their imagination even more, set your child restrictions, such as, "You can paint what you like but you can only use a small square sponge." You will be surprised at what they come up with! You can make collages with different materials, cut up and stuck in a way so as to make a picture using various fabrics, beads, foil and so on for a variety of textures.

Junk modelling: Collect cereal boxes, straws, yogurt pots, paper, wrappers and anything you would ordinarily throw out. These can be used imaginatively to construct almost anything such as a mosque, a vehicle or even a model village. Once everything is glued together in place, then it can be painted and decorated. You can take pictures of your child's work or display it in the house to make them feel good about what they have achieved.

Clay: Clay is a very tactile material and is sure to provide endless amusement for your child. They can model the clay into a sculpture or bowl or pot. Once it has dried there is the opportunity to paint and decorate it. Let your child be creative in what they make and what colours they use. A good alternative if you cannot get hold of clay is playdoh.

Materials: Expose your child to a variety of materials and use descriptive words while you talk about them, such as smooth, shiny, rough, patterned etc. You can even go a bit further with an older child and use this simple sink or float exercise to demonstrate elementary physics. Fill a large bowl with water (or the sink, basin or bath). Fill it with everyday objects such as cotton wool, a paper boat, loose change, a metal spoon and a plastic toy. Get your child to put these in the water and let them tell you what they see. Ask them questions to encourage them to think about what is happening and why.

Construction Blocks: Your child will experiment with stacking the blocks in different ways to create different shapes, horizontally and vertically. Talk to them about what they have created. If, for example, the blocks they have stacked keep falling over and they can't make the building they want, then help your child balance the blocks better and encourage them to build something using this new skill.

Magnets: Your child will have lots of fun with brightly coloured magnets. You can get letter or number magnets that your child can play with to form words and number sequences. But you can take this a bit further and let them explore the properties of magnets. Let them work out that the magnet will stick to the fridge but not to the wooden door. It will stick to keys and cutlery but not to their plastic toys.

Creative with words: Once your child's language skills are more developed then you can encourage them to be creative with words as well. Let them use their thinking, language and hearing by sitting and closing their eyes in the garden and listening to all the noises they can hear. Then ask them to write a poem about the sounds they remember and what that reminds them of. Another good way to be creative with words is to make up stories. They can be based on something you have read together or something you have done together recently as a family.

✏ PHYSICAL DEVELOPMENT

Physical development covers a range of skills from walking to holding a pencil. The physical activities that use more of the body such as running and jumping are called the gross motor skills whereas smaller movement such as those using the fingers are termed fine motor skills. It is important for your child to develop normally in both areas in order to be mobile and independent for their everyday needs. You can help develop your child's motor skills by:

Outdoor play: Incorporate plenty of outdoor physical activity and play into your child's daily routine, for example, flying a kite or any ball sports.

Indoor play: Develop an exercise routine with moves such as sit ups, star jumps and squats that your child can do indoors when they cannot get outside.

Obstacle Course: An obstacle course is the perfect way to develop a number of skills at the same time such as locomotion, balance and co-ordination. You can do this indoors or outdoors and use whatever is at hand, such as chairs, beanbags, hula hoops, boxes and skipping ropes. If there are several children then they can have a race.

Household skills: If you find it hard to attend to your children as well as carrying out your household chores, then your child can join in and help you and improve their motor skills at the same time. For example, they can help clear things away or wash small dishes. Your child will also enjoy cooking, and baking is often the best way to get them involved. They can knead dough, roll out pastry, use cutters to cut out shapes and decorate their efforts. They can also help you in the garden with simple tasks, such as sweeping up a small area.

Tracing: Give your child the opportunity to trace over shapes and letters of the alphabet using a pencil or pen that they can grip properly. With practice, you will see that your child's pencil control improves from random scribbles to writing.

Salah: *Salah* itself has specific gentle yet effective physical movements:

> **Whatever beings there are in the heaves and the earth do prostrate themselves to Allah...** (Surah ar-Rad 13:15)

You can recite this *ayah* to your child emphasising the word *prostration*, what it means and how to do it.

At all times, make sure that your child can express their needs: do they need a rest or a drink after activity? Are they hungry? Help them to make healthy food choices by giving them appropriate snacks. Ask them questions that help them to be aware of their bodies such as, "Can you feel your heart beat faster after you have been running?" "Do you feel hotter after you have been playing?" Explain that this is the way that Allah has designed the amazing human body.

▭ PERSONAL, SOCIAL AND EMOTIONAL DEVELOPMENT

Being social is part of the *sunnah* and it is important to recognise that it is a skill that needs to be developed in your child. Meeting and communicating with people on different levels is part and parcel of everyday life. However, it is the way in which we do this that reveals our character. It is important to teach your child, directly and through example, that they must treat everyone with respect and as they would like to be treated themselves. Show your child that loving someone means, at the very least, spending time with them, being generous to them and helping them remember Allah. There are numerous Qur'an and *hadith* references about a Muslim's duty to others, of which this is only one:

> **The believers are but a single Brotherhood: so make peace and reconciliation between your two (contending) brothers; and fear Allah, that you may receive Mercy.** (Surah al-Hujurat 49:10)

Your child is a unique little individual with feelings and emotions of their own. It is important to recognise this and encourage the normal expression of these feelings. Give your child the opportunity to be as independent as their age allows, let them choose the clothes they want to wear today, give them an either/or choice of what they would like to eat or what activities they would like to do next. Consultation was an important part of how the Prophet ﷺ reached decisions and, although it may seem that your child is too young, it will set a pattern for open mutual communication if you consult with them about seemingly trivial matters now.

You can help your child socialise by ensuring that they spend a balanced amount of time in the company of children their own age as well as older children and adults, but do ensure that they are not ignored or overlooked if there are no children of their own age in a gathering. When a number of children do get together, ensure that they have a constructive activity to concentrate on rather than just jumping on the beds and running around. You can make a mini obstacle course from chairs and sheets or let them share some toys. A good way to improve their confidence in speaking is to sit them down in a circle and tell everyone else about the most recent thing they have learned. This could be a story, *surah*, *ayah* or *kalimah*.

Your child will experience a range of emotions just as you do, but may need help to express them as they may not know how to express themselves. It is perfectly normal for children to be frustrated, angry or sad, but as the adult, you must help them to understand the way they feel, allow them to let it out of their system in a controlled way and then to move on. These activities will help:

Playdoh: This is the child's version of a stress ball! Let your child take out their pent up emotions by squeezing and stretching playdoh.

Drawing with colours: Because children have limited language skills, an effective way to allow your child to express their emotions is through painting and drawing. Tell them, "I want you to draw how you feel, use any colours you want" and then allow them free rein to produce what they like on the page. After they have finished you can ask them questions about what they have drawn which can be the starting point for a conversation about how they feel. At the end of the session, encourage your child to draw something happy so that the experience ends positively and their minds do not dwell on the negative. In this way they have learned, insha'Allah, that it is good to get emotion out of the system and to move on.

Story books: Another effective method of opening up your child's emotions is to read a story with them that contains a character whose facial expressions show different emotions, or a story that mirrors your child's situation. For example, you may have just had a baby. You can share a story with your child about a girl who has a new baby sister but is feeling left out and jealous. Ask your child if they feel that way as well. Ask them open-ended questions relating the little girl in the story to your child. In this way, your child will feel that they are not bad or wrong for feeling the way they do and will appreciate your empathy. You can even finish in the same way that the book ends, so if the little girl gets a present from her baby sister, perhaps you could do the same for your child.

Value things: Try not to throw things away unnecessarily but put them into recycling boxes or give them to charity shops and local swaps. Your child will not mind playing with toys that have been used by another child, because children are not conscious of whether their things are new or branded. As they grow they will learn to appreciate and look after the possessions that they have and understand the value of sharing. This is important in a world where the emphasis is on (over) consumption and materialism.

✎ ISLAMIC DEVELOPMENT

An important part of any Muslim child's curriculum is learning the basic teachings of the *deen* of which the following are a starting point:

1 The Concept of Allah and *Tawheed*
2 The *Kalimahs* and what they mean
3 Faith in Detail (*Iman Mufassil*), Faith in Brief (*Iman Mujmal*), explaining each section – Angels, Books, Messengers, Day of Judgement, Fate (good and bad)
4 The Five Pillars of Islam
5 Short *surahs*
6 Daily *du'as*

To begin with, you can repeat words and phrases to your baby such as Allah and *la illaha illallah*. As your child grows older and develops greater understanding, you can add more details. Use analogies, colourful drawings, pictures, books and posters to explain and help them memorise. Children are never too young to learn and be exposed to the Qur'an. Babies can listen to various melodious recitations. You can teach older children the Arabic alphabet, Arabic sounds and simple words when they can start to understand language. In this way they will find it easy and quick to memorise things in Arabic.

The important thing is to make religious learning as exciting and relevant as any other subject and a little effort to organise the following activities will ensure that your child looks forward to their Islam learning time.

Voice recording: Record your child's voice when they recite the Qur'an or *du'as*. They can learn from their mistakes and improve quickly in this way. In fact this can be done by the whole family.

Competitions: You can hold gentle competitions between children to encourage them to learn more. For example, you can ask two or more children to learn the first ten names of the 99 names of Allah. The faster child gets a bigger gift and the slower child gets a slightly smaller gift. They are both winners, as they have learnt something valuable. Similarly you can do this with a small *surah* or *du'a*.

Group Activities: Invite a number of children round for a gathering and organise activities for them. It is good for children to be with like-minded company and children do tend to learn more quickly from each other. Remember to keep things light and fun. Perhaps you can organise a talk about manners, rights of parents or someone to tell them stories of the Prophets. Enlist the help of the other parents for ideas and pool together everyone's skills and talents for the benefit of the children.

Matching words: Flash cards are a very useful way to learn words and language. You can make Islamic flash cards in Arabic or English (or whatever other language your child speaks). You can have your child match words to pictures or Arabic word to English word or match two similar words from the Qur'an such as olive and fig, elephant and ant, prayer and Makkah.

Reading clubs: You could set up a reading club where children and their parents read a book every month. Each month all the children in the club get together and discuss their favourite part led by an adult. You can introduce stories of the Prophets, notable male and female Muslim role models. The stories need to be simple and not so long that the children lose concentration.

Islam is a way of life, a state or condition of the heart. While there is much that you will be able to teach your child, the real essence of Islam can only be understood by a child following your example. The best way to ensure the best Islamic development for your child is to embody Islam, the Qur'an and *Sunnah* as much as possible in your everyday actions and words, as mentioned previously. You must be aware of establishing *salah* five times a day, of fulfilling the rights of the people around you, right down to removing an object from the road so as not to harm people. Your actions, speech, eating, drinking, mannerisms, dress must all be for the pleasure of Allah and only then will your child follow your lead.

In short:

⇒ Ensure that you develop your child's skills in all areas, not just their areas of strength.

⇒ Provide a range of resources and learning opportunities for your child to benefit from.

⇒ Try to incorporate your child's interests when doing an activity with them.

⇒ Incorporate Islam into as many areas as possible.

CHAPTER EIGHT

PLANNING YOUR DAY AND ACTIVITIES

Your mind is probably buzzing with ideas of what activities you would like to do with your child and you are filled with good intentions. But what is the next step? It is important to spend a bit of time getting organised and writing everything down. It may seem like a waste of your valuable time, but it is worth it in the long run.

Develop a daily plan. This should be very simple and basic to start with but will help you to focus on the time you have and the range of activities that you can do with your child in a given period of time.

Develop a detailed plan. Add more detail to the basic plan, such as the nature of the activities that you plan to carry out and your aim in doing so.

Prepare activities. Make a note of the materials you will need for each activity, where you will get them from, what arrangements you need to make to carry out that activity and so on.

✏️ DEVELOPING A DAILY PLAN

Planning a day can be difficult especially as so many things just 'pop up' during the week. At this stage, just divide the day into three sections and write down one or two activities in each. Make your curriculum flexible, creative and be realistic as to what you are able to carry out; don't overdo things. Use the wider environment and consider talking to your family and friends for ideas for your curriculum plan.

Remember that your plan is a general guide to help put some structure into your child's day (and yours!) and a means of putting on paper what you hope to achieve with them. If something urgent comes up and you are unable to do an activity on the plan, then that's alright. Similarly, if you have planned Qur'an lessons for your child but they are in a disruptive mood, then switch to a creative or outdoor activity to get the excess energy out of their system. You can do that Qur'an lesson later in the week.

You can change the plan around every few weeks and introduce new activities when your child is ready and you feel that they need some variety. The best guide to knowing when to change activities on your plan is by observing your child's responses and reactions over time.

If you have different aged children there is no need to make two plans, unless you want to. For example talking about the Prophet Muhammad ﷺ can be extended for a 5-year-old and kept simple for a 3-year-old.

Another thing to remember is that all sorts of activities can go on the plan, such as, cooking, shopping and going to people's houses. These are all learning opportunities if you present them to your child·in that way. For example, you may feel that a trip to the market to go shopping is a mundane chore. But you can make it exciting and educational by:

» Playing a number game or reciting a *du'a* in the car.
» Teaching your child the name of a new fruit or vegetable each time you go, in Arabic and English.
» Pointing out the different produce that is in season.
» Asking your child to help you pick out an item from the shelf and put it into your basket.
» Involving your child in simple decisions: "Would you like green apples or red apples this time?"
» When you come home, they can help you put things away and then write or draw about their experience. You can encourage them to talk about their work with a sibling or parent who did not accompany them on the trip.

This is an example of a very basic daily plan, which is more of a note to yourself to improvise and extend as needed:

	Morning	Afternoon	Evening
Monday	shopping	creative	Islam
Tuesday	problem solving	physical	language
Wednesday	knowledge of the world	personal/social	play date with friends
Thursday	creative	Islam	problem solving
Friday	Islam	go to mosque	play with cousins
Saturday	personal/ social	knowledge of the world	physical
Sunday	language	spend time with dad in the garden/park	spend time together as a whole family

✏ DETAILED ACTIVITY PLAN

Now you have some basic structure to your days, you can think a bit more about how you are going to put this into action. Have a little brainstorming session about what you can do. This, for example, is what you might put for 'language'.

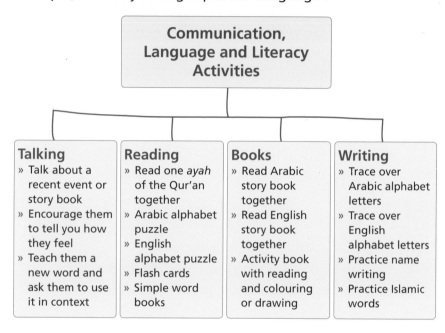

Now all you have to do is replace 'language' with one of the activities. Similarly you can develop a detailed plan for each area of the curriculum. It is worth spending some time over this stage as one activity can cover many aspects of the same area of the curriculum as well as other developmental skills. You will need some quiet time during the day when you are not disturbed to get ideas and inspiration. You can also get guidance from the internet, other parents and even from your child themselves. What do they show an interest in and how can you make it educational and interesting for them?

If you would like to go one step further, you can develop a weekly plan with activities that centre around a theme. This theme can be carried through all the activities for a week and insha'Allah your child will benefit from a detailed understanding of that theme. For example in spring or autumn when it is raining almost every day, you could pick the theme of rain and your weekly example could look something like this:

THEME: RAIN

Communication, Language and Literacy
» Go to the library and get a book on rain; read it together.
» Practice writing the words: rain, wet, water.
» Learn about the water cycle, making diagrams and writing about it.

Problem Solving, Reasoning and Numeracy
» Draw a cloud with rain drops and count the drops.
» Make a rain gauge by cutting the top off a plastic mineral water bottle. Mark off 1cm increments on the handle of a wooden spoon and put the spoon upside down into the water bottle. Put the rain gauge outside and measure how much it has rained.

Knowledge and Understanding of the World
» Look at where and why there are puddles after rain.
» Look at animals that come out in the rain (e.g. snails) and why others hide.
» Get a world map and look at countries with the least and greatest rainfall and compare their landscapes.

Creative

» Make hats for rainy days.
» Use sheets and chairs to make pretend tents indoors.
» Use wet painting/water colours on wet paper and see how the paint colours run into each other.

Physical

» Put on waterproof hats, coats and wellies. Play outside and splash on puddles once the rain has settled down.

Personal, Social, Emotional

» Talk about how your child feels when it rains.
» Talk about storms and lightening. Do these scare your child? Reassure them and ask them to trust in Allah.

Islam

» Talk about how and why Allah created the rain e.g. to help plants grow. Look up an *ayah* from the Qur'an about rain and how Allah brings the earth to life.
» Read the *ahadith* that deal with rain and the *du'as* that can be recited when it rains.
» It is *sunnah* to make *du'a* when it rains and also to get a little wet as it is a blessing from Allah.

✏️ PREPARING ACTIVITIES

For each activity, you will need to write down what you need and where you can get these from. It is worth investing in some basic and much used equipment, such as, a plastic apron, paint brushes, crayons, sugar paper, exercise books, folders, play mats etc. These will come in useful time and time again. You may also need to re-arrange the space to do your activity. For example, painting with fingers and feet may require you to clear away a large area of space, lay down plastic sheets and have bowls of water and towels to hand.

Ensure that you have everything you need before starting an activity so that the activity can run smoothly and without interruption. The more prepared you are for the activities, the more you and your child can get out of them in a relaxed and enjoyable manner.

✏️ OTHER POINTS TO REMEMBER

» Children find it hard to focus and remain attentive for long periods of time. Do be sure to make sessions interesting for them and keep them short.

» Health and safety should be of paramount importance. Never leave your child unattended and pay close attention to what they are doing at all times. Make sure that all the equipment you use is in good, working order and that it is suitable to be used by children e.g. blunt ended scissors, non-toxic paints etc.

» One activity can cover more than one aspect of the curriculum. For example, a session may involve drawing a picture of a tree with apples, writing a few words about it, and talking about it. Here we have covered: creative (drawing), language (writing and talking), numeracy (counting the apples on the tree) and Islam (talking about Allah's creation).

» Allow your child the opportunity to learn about a variety of topics. Don't worry if you are not too confident about a particular subject. You can always look up more about it on the internet or go to the library for more information. This will expand your knowledge and your child will learn from you how to gather information from various sources. It is also a useful lesson in understanding that there is no shame in not always knowing the answer, admitting that there is a gap in knowledge and doing something about it.

» When you talk to your child, do remember to be patient with them. They will appreciate you taking the time out to explain things to them and help them understand. On the other hand, there is no need to be long-winded with your explanations and advice as the child will just lose interest. The Prophet Muhammad ﷺ maintained a balance between these two extremes. He was very much straight to the point and whatever advice or lessons he would give would be of direct and relevant benefit.

The best of knowledge is that which is beneficial. (Bukhari)

In short:

✏ Develop a basic weekly plan followed by a more detailed plan. This should fit in with your daily chores and number of children.

✏ Thoroughly plan your activities in advance making sure you have all the materials that you need.

✏ Bear in mind what you are aiming for with each activity.

✏ Be prepared to be flexible with your plan and to change it if your child is not responding positively to it.

✏ Have fun!

CHAPTER NINE

OBSERVING YOUR CHILD

It may sound trivial but it is important to spend time observing your child. Watch them while they are at play, try to establish their strengths and weaknesses, their likes and dislikes and how they approach issues. Understandably, with the number of tasks that parents are continually juggling, it is not always easy to find the time to sit and do this, but it will pay off. It will allow you to learn more about your child and how best you can meet their needs as a parent.

Observations can help you to:

» See how your child is progressing with specific tasks;
» Check their overall development;
» Pick up on problems that your child may have;
» Think about how best to resolve these problems based on your previous observations;
» Develop plans and strategies for future activities and routines;
» Learn and understand more about your child's personality and nature.

You can either choose to keep several files or one large file which you sub-divide into sections. Each section or file should correspond with one subject in the curriculum that you are currently working on with your child and should contain your notes as well as samples of your child's work in chronological order. In this way it is easy to keep track of their progress, for example, in handwriting or artwork.

There are a number of methods that are used by childcare professionals to record their observations about children. However, if you wish to make notes about the progress of your child for your own records then you can simply write down what you see. With a little practice and experience it will become second nature. Here are a few points to get you started:

» Ensure that your child does not realise you are observing them as this may affect their behaviour.
» You can still get involved with your child but obviously this means that it will be harder for you to write things down at the time.

» Decide what it is that you want to observe. For example, you may wish to record your daughter's fine motor skills. You would observe her when she is trying to button her coat, draw a picture or thread beads through string.
» You would note down the manner in which she attempted this, whether she was successful, her facial expression, mannerisms and actions.

Here is an example of an entry for fine motor skills for a two-year-old girl.

To observe... Fine motor skills (physical development)
Date: 07/05/2010   Name: Safiyyah
Observation: Safiyyah is attempting to button her coat up. She gets frustrated and shows this by getting angry at herself. Later she is given some Arabic letters to trace over. She holds the pencil in her right hand with good grip and the correct position. She is unable to trace over the letters and makes random scribbles on the page.

From the first part of this observation, you can see that Safiyyah has difficulty in buttoning up her coat and when she is unsuccessful, she gets angry. Therefore, she needs help with doing up her buttons as well as help to control her frustration. You can follow up this observation in these ways:
» Praise her for trying to button her coat by herself. Encourage her by saying that she is almost there and will insha'Allah be able to do it next time.
» Stay calm and soothing while she is angry.

» Explain that it is not helpful to get angry and that this will only make the task harder.
» Give her further activities to help her fine motor skills such as threading beads through a shoe lace. Give her something simple to start with that she is sure to succeed at, in order to develop her confidence. Then give her progressively harder tasks, encouraging and praising at each stage until this no longer remains an issue.

The second part of the observation shows that Safiyyah has a good pencil grip, but cannot trace over letters. This would be followed up by:
» Praising her for holding her pencil well.
» Understanding that she may not be ready to trace over letters and so give her more basic shapes to trace over such as a large square, circle and triangle.
» Including other activities in her day such drawing and cutting out shapes that will help to develop her hand-eye coordination.
» Once she has mastered this and gained confidence, then give her the Arabic alphabet to trace over.
» You can photocopy several sheets of the Arabic alphabet and give her one every week or so. By putting the date in the corner and filing these in date order, you will have a lovely record of how your child has developed from making random scribbles on the page to an almost exact trace of the letters. Practice makes perfect!

With this so-called 'free description' method, you can gain a lot of information to help your child progress or develop. You will even find yourself helping with skills that you did not even plan to observe in the first place. The main thing is that the observation does not have to be long or detailed. It should be a few simple sentences that you can glance through later and use to formulate your plan for the next stage. This tailored approach will help your child develop to the best of their potential in the shortest period of time, insha'Allah, and the most rewarding part for you, as the parent, is to see how you helped them along in that journey.

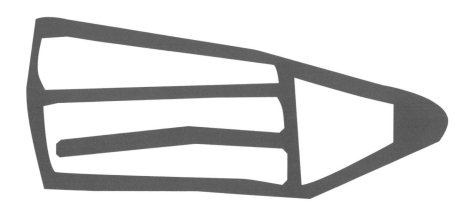